D0209425

Dark Threads
the
Weaver Needs

Dark Threads the Weaver Needs

Herbert Lockyer

Fleming H. Revell Company
Old Tappan, New Jersey

Library of Congress Cataloging in Publication Data

Lockyer, Herbert.
    Dark threads the weaver needs.

    1. Suffering. I. Title.
BT732.7.L63   242'.4   78-11620
ISBN 0-8007-0977-2

TO all
who suffer nobly
according to the will of God

Contents

Preface: A Mirror or a Window? 11

1 "I Sat Where They Sat" 15

2 Every Heart Bears a Mark 27

3 Dark Threads the Weaver Needs 35

4 Harmony Between Attributes and Action 49

5 Godliness Does Not Guarantee Immunity 61

6 How to Meet Suffering 85

7 Beside the Waters of Comfort 97

8 Where Eyes Are Never Wet With Tears 113

. . . why art thou so far from helping me,
and from the words of my roaring?

Psalms 22:1

Preface: A Mirror or a Window?

Have you ever stopped to think of the great difference between a window and a mirror? In a mirror you see only yourself, but through a window you do not see yourself but others. From looking at a single face, you look out upon a sea of faces. Too many give a great amount of time to the mirror. If only they spent as much time on their knees in prayer for others, they would cultivate an inner and facial beauty attractive to all around. Suffering, it would seem, puts either a window or a mirror in one's life. Some dear people meet suffering by taking out the window and substituting a mirror. In their trial and grief they become introspective, morbid, and self-pitying. They see only their sorrow, their need, their pain, their urgency, their injustice. They have not learned to sing:

> Go bury thy sorrow,
> The world hath its share.
>
> PHILIP BLISS

On the other hand, there are those unselfish hearts who, in the time of anguish and calamity, take out the mirror and replace it with a window, in order to see the needs of others around them. Thus, with new vision, their own experience of suffering can be made a blessing. How we triumph when we realize that we cannot live as unto Him who lived and died for others without the window sufferings brings. Without windows, the great bonds of sympathy and understanding that sweep around the world would be impossible. In national life we are proud of our democracy. There is a great democracy in suffering, for we all share in it, and are meant to help each other by it. It was for our sakes that Jesus sanctified and sacrificed Himself. God means for us, then, to look out of a window on the world, and not waste time gazing at our own personal sorrow.

> Hearts growing a-weary
>   With heavier woe,
> Now droop 'mid the darkness—
>   Go, comfort them, go!
> Go, bury thy sorrows,
>   Let others be blest;
> Go, give them the sunshine:
>   Tell Jesus the rest.
>
> **PHILIP BLISS**

Love suffereth long, and is kind to others, and the longer love suffers, the kinder it becomes toward those who have a heavy load to carry. Love suffers long, because it suffers deeply. Percy C. Ainsworth has reminded us that "the long-suffering of love is just the negative side of its service to others. Its kindness is the positive side of that service." We recognize that suffering is disciplinary and corrective, redeeming our faults by measures as mild as possible, and is a sign, not of God's displeasure, but His love. "For whom the Lord loveth he chasteneth . . ." (Hebrews 12:6). The divine purpose of suffering does not end with ourselves but is meant to be a channel of blessing to others—personal holiness, then service for others. The trial of our faith is much more precious than gold when it enriches other lives as well as our own.

What we must not forget is that the amount of hidden sorrow in the world is incalculable. Human suffering is like an iceberg—nine-tenths of it is not seen. Some of the greatest sufferers possess the gift of silence, hiding their secret till they die. If those who hide their sorrow revealed it, the world would be a most unhappy place in which to live. One is a genius if he can read the history of a suffering soul in a human face. If we would gather gain for our pain, then we must ask God to give us that love, having second sight, so that we can see behind the veil camouflaging pain, and become comforters to those who try to conceal it. If we fail in this blessed task, then our sorrow is a lost sorrow.

1

"I Sat Where They Sat"

Blest Be the Tie

Blest be the tie that binds
  Our hearts in Christian love;
The fellowship of kindred minds
  Is like to that above.

Before our Father's throne
  We pour our ardent prayers;
Our fears, our hopes, our aims are one,
  Our comforts and our cares.

We share our mutual woes,
  Our mutual burdens bear;
And often for each other flows
  The sympathizing tear.

When we asunder part,
  It gives us inward pain;
But we shall still be joined in heart,
  And hope to meet again.

This glorious hope revives
  Our courage by the way,
While each in expectation lives,
  And waits to see the day.

From sorrow, toil, and pain,
  And sin, we shall be free,
And perfect love and friendship reign
  Through all eternity.

JOHN FAWCETT

In the bondage of babylon, the prophet Ezekiel wrote a simple phrase which expresses volumes of unspoken consolation: ". . . I sat where they sat . . ." (Ezekiel 3:15). The prophet did not offer condolence from afar. He was right there suffering along with those in captivity at Tel-abib. His shared sufferings fitted him to minister as Jehovah's watchman to his fellow captives. Ezekiel exhibited sympathy—a mental and personal participation in another's trouble, a kindred or like feeling.

There is a world of difference between *sympathy* and *sorrow*. We can have genuine sorrow for a friend facing heartbreak over some crushing trial or disappointment without the personal experience of what such a friend may be passing through, but we cannot have *sympathy* for him unless we have sat where he is sitting. *Sym* means "with," and *pathy* is from *pathos,* meaning "pain" or "sufferings." Thus the word implies suffering with another, or the capacity of entering into the feelings or experience of a sufferer.

Sympathy is born in the womb of experience. Much comfort often comes to a sufferer from the touch of a friendly hand and a few simple words, quietly and kindly spoken, such as, "God bless you, friend; I know just how you feel, for I·have been through the very same thing."

There is a close relationship between *symphony* and *sympathy*. The former speaks of the harmony of instrumental sounds; the latter speaks of that harmony which makes suffering hearts one. In the introduction to his moving volume *Christ and Human Suffering*, E. Stanley Jones has this most gripping paragraph:

> To write on such a subject is to walk on holy ground, hallowed by tears and blood-stained footsteps of many a wearied one. To bungle here would be serious. To raise hopes in a suffering breast that could not be fulfilled would only add pain to pain. I hesitated. But objection after objection seemed to be swept away, and I came to the final condition and took my stand there, refusing to go on unless I could be assured at this point. *I cannot write this book as theory.* It must be a working way to live. I have learned something of this Secret, and it has been glorious: but I can write on this subject only on one condition that "You teach me, Father, to walk in this way, and to walk in it with abandon, as I try to unfold it to others."

Those acquainted with this remarkable treatise on suffering will know how well this missionary-author succeeded in ladling out of the crucible of experience such precious literary gold. Many of us find it hard to believe that we cannot *bless* unless we *bleed*. One meaning the dictionary gives of *bleed* is "to feel the pain or anguish of another." The broken heart of Jesus reveals how deeply touched He was with our infirmities and how tested He was in all points *just as we are* (Hebrews 2:9–18; 4:15). A glorious aspect of His Incarnation was His willingness to leave the painless world of heaven and come to a world of tears to sit where sufferers sat. Through the centuries, countless multitudes of lives crushed and broken by sin and suffering have been blessedly saved and restored through Calvary's bleeding heart.

> O Saviour Christ, Thou too art Man;
> Thou hast been troubled, tempted, tried;
> Thy kind but searching glance can scan
> The very wounds that shame would hide.
> "At Even, When the Sun Did Set"
> HENRY TWELLS

If the proverb be true that "he who suffers most has most to give," then the Man of Sorrows had more to give than any other. There was never any sorrow and suffering like unto His. Does it not amaze us to read that, although He was the Son of God, He learned obedience by the things He suffered (Hebrews 5:8, 9)? This is why He can offer eternal salvation to all who tread the same path of obedience. As the Bread born, He had to be bruised before He could become food for the hungry.

Are we following the steps of the Master's example in bleeding to bless? Have we learned that some of the inexplicable trials we faced did not prove that God is *not,* but that *His is* and that, through them He was fitting us, not only to carry out His will, but to reveal to others His Son's submission to the divine will? Did He not teach His disciples that His purging of them was designed to make them more fruitful in life and service? Passing through fire and water we come out into a wealthy place. Fellowship in suffering enriches our own character and fits us to reach others with the consolation of the Gospel. It has been said that "the furnace and the anvil and the hammer are essential to the strength and beauty of the metal that is being shaped under the craftsman's hand." Yet we are so slow to learn that divine love permits us to be chastised in order that we might become partakers of divine holiness, and through such holiness lead others, who are being chastened, to experience the same blessed life.

Shelley says of poets, "They learn in suffering what they teach in song." Sarah (Sadie) Williams, poet of the eighteenth century, left us the lines:

> The mark of rank in nature is capacity for pain,
> And the anguish of the singer marks the sweet-
> ness of the strain.

The song born of suffering is the only one we can sing for the comfort of others. George Meredith, famous English poet, affirmed that "there is nothing the body suffers that the soul may not profit by." The bodily and mental sufferings the Apostle Paul endured gave him a song so richly blessed to pass on to afflicted hearts all down the ages. We must, like Paul, become scholars in the school of sympathy if we would be able to ". . . comfort those who are in any affliction . . ." (2 Corinthians 1:4, RSV).

The lowly yet precious marine mollusk—the pearl oyster—can teach us a most profitable lesson on how to transform pain into a pearl, or irritation into irradiation. The lining of the shell of oyster is made of mother-of-pearl which provides a smooth surface against its body. The pearls some oysters produce are of the same material.

Pearls are produced by these small handsomeless creatures in their efforts to get rid of, or to kill, a minute worm, or some other irritating object such as a grain of sand. By repeated action the secretions of the mother-of-pearl become layers of considerable thickness and what had pained the oyster becomes a pearl. But man has come along to help the mollusk in the making of these gems. A grain or so of sand or a tiny piece of mother-of-pearl is inserted between the shell and the outer skin of the oyster, and when opened after some two or three years, the *cultured* pearl is found. Such a method must cause the creature to suffer to some degree, but through its constant tears, or secretions, the oyster gives back a pearl for pain. Man gives the poor creature much suffering but patient endurance changes the unwelcome irritation into an object of wealth and value.

Are not God's pearls—He calls them His jewels—cultured in the same way? Irritating trials, often inflicted by others and divinely permitted, cause us inward pain and tend to produce doubt and despair. But if we, like the oyster, seek to enrich those who injure us, then we must learn how to coat our suffering with tears, faith in Him, and submission to His all-wise purpose. In this way, by His grace and power, disaster or disease can be transformed into a pearl whose luster glorifies God.

After such a preamble, the reader wants to ask the writer whether he has sat where others sit, whether he writes as an onlooker or participant, whether he is a graduate of the School of Sympathy, whether he has had experiences of pain becoming pearls. In all humility, the qualification I have to author a book on the problems of human suffering is, first of all, my contact with life for ninety-two years.

In His matchless grace, the Lord met and saved me more than seventy-two years ago, and if only I could record the story of these years with their personal trials, heartaches, disappointments, and suffering, you would know how fitted I am to attempt such a volume. Through years in the pastorate, I came close to tragedy, pain, frustrations, diseases, and death in visiting homes and hospitals. Often have I been compelled to ask my own heart as I tried to comfort distressed and perplexed sufferers, *O my God, why?* How exquisite are the lines of Elizabeth Barrett Browning on sympathy:

> I am no trumpet, but a reed,
> A broken reed the wind indeed
>   Left flat upon a dismal shore:
> Yet, if a little maid or child
> Should sigh within it earnest-mild,
>   This reed will answer evermore.

In agreement is the prayer expressed by Anna L. Waring:

> I ask thee for a thoughtful love,
>   Through constant watching wise,
> To meet the glad with joyful smiles,
>   And wipe the weeping eyes,
> A heart at leisure from itself,
>   To soothe and sympathize.

My further qualification is more personal and intimate, and I am reluctant to describe it. My dear wife and I have been married for more than sixty-six years, but through the last seven years or so, she has been practically dead to the world. Mentally afflicted, my lifelong partner has no consciousness of the past or present, is unable to recognize her own dear ones, is speechless, and almost totally blind and deaf, is incontinent, is bedridden and has to be fed like a baby with baby food only. Apart from the daily visit of a nurse who washes and protects her from sores, the care of my helpless one has been my responsibility. Often, as I have looked upon her afflicted, helpless form, I have asked, "O my God, why?" And need I confess it that, occasionally, the prayer ascends to God asking Him to take her if it is His perfect will.

At the time of writing she is ninety-two years of age, and has gradually become weaker and thus it has become difficult to give her the personal care she needs. For well over sixty years, as an evangelist, pastor, a traveling Bible teacher in Britain and America, my life has been predominantly public. But during the last seven years, a complete transformation has come about through my being confined to the house, caring for my loved one and for myself. Wonderfully, God has sustained me and has enabled me to "trace the rainbow through the rain." He, whose permissive will is ever best for His redeemed children, has taught me sympathy, patience, kindness, and compassion.

Not only so, but while being homebound, in between the times of attention my wife requires, I have been able to write several well-known books.

Through meditation born of a clearer understanding of Him who moves in a mysterious way, His wonders to perform, humbly I confess I have a more "thoughtful love, through constant watching wise" and a "heart at leisure from itself to soothe and sympathize." Matson's hymn has a deeper meaning for me now:

> O blessed Life! the heart at rest,
>   When all without tumultuous seems:
>   That trusts a higher Will, and deems
> That higher Will, not mine, the best.

Note: Two days after writing the above lines, my dear one was taken to be with the Lord, forever delivered from the infirmities of the flesh.

2

Every Heart Bears a Mark

There's Not a Grief, However Light

There's not a grief, however light,
Too light for sympathy;
There's not a care, however slight,
Too slight to bring to thee.

Thou who hast trod the thorny road
Wilt share each small distress;
For he who bore the greater load
Will not refuse the less.

There's not a secret sigh we breathe
But meets thine ear divine,
And every cross grows light beneath
The shadow, Lord, of thine.

Life's woes without, sin's strife within,
The heart would overflow,
But for that love which died for sin,
That love which wept with woe.

JANE CREWDSON

WHEREVER MAN OR BEAST are found, there suffering takes its toll for "the *whole* creation groans and travails in pain up to this moment" (*see* Romans 8:19–25).

Ever since the first man existed, every man has been afflicted with suffering of some sort or another. It has been said of the Bible that "without tears it was not written, and without tears it cannot be understood." No one can read its sacred pages without discovering that pain, anguish, and suffering, mysterious to the mind of man, are given prominence. Suffering is as old as sin and vitally connected with it. The sorrows of life that have deluged the world since Adam and Eve are directly or indirectly the fruit of their sin. The whole race has had to share the results of their disobedience to God's command. Sin, sickness, and death followed upon their Fall. ". . . by one man sin entered into the world, and death by sin. . ." (Romans 5:12). As Eve was the first to obey Satan rather than God, woman has been the chief sufferer in the world.

But every heart, since God first created these

marvelous life-giving structures for Adam and Eve, has borne the mark of suffering; and as the population of the earth was never so great as it is today, there are multitudes more sufferers than ever before. And who is able to recount earth's tragedies and calamities: war, famine, pestilence, vandalism, violence, kidnapping, all part of the entail of sin? If "every heart knows its own bitterness," then we have the countless millions of hearts and homes representing a mountain of grief, pain, suffering, disillusionment, and despair. This, all because earth's first home was marred by sin and became the first home to be shadowed by sin, death—and murder!

A haunting question some might raise is, "If God knew that the sin of the first pair He created would result in a world of suffering, pain, woe, and death, why did God not kill the devil when He saw his evil purpose?" While the Creator originally meant and adapted heredity as a channel of blessing, Satan turned it into a channel of cursing. But God is not to be blamed for satanic perversion. When He created man, he was not made as a mere machine with no power of choice. He endowed him with free will, with power to obey or disobey his Creator. The long, long trail of human suffering testifies to the fact that Adam used his freedom in the wrong direction, and none of his descendants have been free from the sad consequences of his wrong choice. Sin arose from within man because of the choice of will.

Our wills are ours, we know not how,
Our wills are ours, to make them thine.

ALFRED TENNYSON

What a different story would have come out of the Garden of Eden if Adam and Eve had made their wills harmonize with God's sweet will! But He did not force them to yield obedience unto Him. When Jesus came as the One delighting to do the will of God, He recognized and respected the freedom and dignity of the human will when He said, "If any man *will to do* My will, he shall know of the doctrine" (*see* John 7:17) and "Ye *will not* come unto Me" (*see* John 5:40). He did not compel men to be saved. He left them to choose whom they would serve.

The bright aspect of the dark tragedy of Eden is that God *did* intervene. As soon as man fell, He announced the first prophecy of salvation for a world that would be full of sinners lost and ruined by the Fall. Through the seed of the first created woman who was the first to disobey and dishonor God, One was to come, born of a woman, to destroy the works of the devil, and provide a perfect salvation for a sinning race. Thus, in Genesis 3:15 we have the first announcement of the blessed evangel, the seed of a woman, who would bruise the serpent's head. If in Adam man must still suffer and die, in Christ he can be made alive, or restored to God and emancipated from sin's guilt and government.

While Calvary made possible deliverance from sin, the root cause of suffering, it does not eliminate all the various types of suffering sin gave birth to. Yet, through Him who suffered under Pontius Pilate, who decreed the Crucifixion of Jesus, a soothing balm for all redeemed by His precious Blood can be had. The righteous are enabled to suffer nobly as they think of Him who was led as a *lamb* to the slaughter—silent and submissive. Through the cross they discover a beauty in suffering, which almost explains and justifies its existence, and wear the flower of pain, blossoming as the result of their sorrow. Like their Master, the greatest of all sufferers, they possess the gift of silence. They bury their own sorrow, for the world has its share.

While the world has no man who has not suffered in some way or another because of Adam's transgression and in experience by his own sin, *suffering* is a general term covering many facets of what man endures. For instance, there are bodily sufferings, mental sufferings, spiritual sufferings, voluntary and vicarious sufferings. A few choice saints exhibit all that is entailed in these different sufferings. Such was the lot of that first-century martyr Ignatius. This renowned church father was brought before the emperor, condemned to death, transported to Rome and thrown among the wild beasts in the Colosseum. Fearing that the Christians in Rome would try to procure his pardon, he wrote them a letter beseeching them to show him no such "unreasonable kindness," and he ended his request on this courageous note:

> Come fire and cross, come crowds of wild beasts; come tearing and mangling, wrecking of bones and hacking of limbs; come cruel torments of the devil, only let me attain unto Jesus Christ.

All who are truly the Lord's should have hearts bearing the mark of voluntary and vicarious suffering, no matter how else they may suffer. Such a phase can be avoided by those who do not desire to enter deeply into the fellowship with Christ in His sufferings (Philippians 3:10). This particular suffering is that into which we voluntarily enter for the sake of intimate fellowship with the Lord, and for abundant service in a world of sin and pain. It is entered in response to His demand, "If any man will come after me, let him deny himself, and take up his cross, and follow me" (*see* Matthew 16:21–27). The voluntary assumption of "the sufferings of Christ" involves the denial of self and identification with Him in a vicarious witness, namely sacrifice for others' sake. A similar lesson is taught in the parable of a corn of wheat which "abides alone" if it does not die. The condition of producing a harvest is burial—and, alas! too few of us are prepared to suffer and die in the way the Lord of the Harvest sets forth.

3

Dark Threads the Weaver Needs

The Divine Weaver

My Life is but a weaving
　Between my Lord and me;
I cannot choose the colours
　He worketh steadily.

Ofttimes He weaveth sorrow
　And I in foolish pride,
Forget that He seeth the upper,
　And I the under side.

Not till the loom is silent
　And the shuttles cease to fly,
Shall God unroll the canvas
　And explain the reason why.

The dark threads are as needful
　In the Weaver's skillful hand,
As the threads of gold and silver
　In the pattern He has planned.

AUTHOR UNKNOWN

THE DESERVED SUFFERING of godless, evil-minded persons presents no mystery. Overtaken in pain and anguish, they reap what they have sown. Throughout Scripture the principle of penal and judicial suffering, as a form of just retribution, is clearly taught. Such a penalty upon evildoers operates because of the demand of a righteous law and an inflexibly just Judge. ". . . every transgression and disobedience received a just recompense of reward" (Hebrews 2:2). If it were otherwise, then God Himself would become a partner in sin. But the consistent declaration is that because of God's righteous government, no evildoer can escape the suffering his evil deeds merit.

But while the suffering a sinner causes others is visited upon his own pate (Psalms 7:16), why are those who do not merit suffering left to endure so much of it? A question often asked is, "Why does a righteous God permit the righteous to suffer?" Many of the godly in Christ Jesus have moments of perplexity over the undeserved pain they are given to endure, and from a despairing heart cry, "O God, why?" The troubled one cannot see how the dark threads are as needful in the divine Weaver's plan. Eager to live in accordance with God's will for his life, and strongly adverse to indulging in any known sin, he is mystified when his hopes are crushed and his castles fall.

Uncertainty as to the significance of God's permissive will often produces much mental and spiritual suffering. But what if Christians were infallibly spared from pain and sorrow? Would this not be a degradation of all that is truly called Christian? E. Stanley Jones illustrates this folly by saying that "the head of a school who enrolled his own child in his own school but exempted the child from the operations of the disciplines and penalties of the school would do himself, his child, and the school a distinct and serious harm." Apart, then, from those recognized sufferings incidental to human life and living, there are dark and sudden calamities that leave us stunned and shaken. And as our universe seems to tumble in on us, faith in God receives a deep shock.

A dear Christian relative of mine was left a widow early in her married life. One day, her husband and their young son went out for a row. A squall arose; the boat capsized; and father and son were drowned. The sudden catastrophe left the young widow and mother asking, "If there is a personal God who loves me, why did He not save me from this tragedy?"

To suffer as the result of one's own inner choice

and action is one thing, but why should some suffer when they do not choose or merit such sufferings? The heart asks for an answer. It is accepted that the wicked reap what they sow, because sin ever leaves its imprint, and brings forth a harvest of grief and sorrow. But why was such a godly man as Stephen, full of faith and the Holy Spirit, permitted to become the first martyr of the church when an angry mob brutally stoned him to death?

C. H. Spurgeon, prince of preachers, wrote and preached a great deal about suffering, merited and unmerited, and of the sufficiency of God's grace when the godly are called upon to suffer. Yet this marvelous winner of souls, toward the close of his remarkable ministry, never knew a day without physical pain. On the large pulpit of his London church was a couch where he lay during the preliminary part of the service conducted by a helper and prayed for strength and grace from on high to preach the Gospel as only he could. Then, having delivered his soul, back to the couch he went. We can imagine hundreds of the congregation asking why God allowed His most faithful and useful servant to suffer so, when he was so bent on honoring Him by life, lip, and literature.

How true it is that some of the choicest saints on earth are often among the greatest sufferers! Fanny Crosby, the famous hymn writer, had to sit in darkness during nearly all of her long, devoted life. Yet the unforgettable hymns of this blind hymnist reveal no sign of complaint.

A certain master maker of fine violins was said to choose the wood for his instruments from the north side of trees, and it would seem as if God finds most of His choicest examples of godliness on life's north side. Yet, somehow it is so hard for some godly sufferers to experience the gain in their pain, and in life's dark hours theirs is the desperate cry, *"Why is God silent? Why does He not intervene?"*

Thomas Carlyle gave fresh utterance to a perplexity as old as time when, meditating on some of life's enigmas, he exclaimed petulantly: "The worst of God is that He does nothing."

David cried: "Lord, how long wilt thou look on? . . ." (Psalms 35:17). And the prophet Habakkuk prayed to God when so heavily burdened: ". . . wherefore lookest thou upon them that deal treacherously, and holdest thy tongue . . . ?" (1:13).

Today as we read of disastrous floods and famines, cyclones and earthquakes, wars and national crises, lawlessness and crime, and the utter inability of rulers to rule, is it any wonder perplexed and impatient hearts ask, "Why does God not intervene?" Personal tragedies and calamities call forth the same question.

We lose sight of the fact that certain assumptions are implicit in such a question. First of all, it recognizes that there is a God to intervene, otherwise the question would be meaningless. Second, the question implies that God has an interest in men, otherwise His intervention in their affairs would not be expected. In the third place, the question assumes that He has the ability to intervene and end the problems of universal and personal suffering. Fourth, implicit in the question is, seeing He is Almighty God, He *ought* to intervene. If it is right and proper that He should reveal His power and authority, why does He not do so?

Those troubled about God's nonintervention in the affairs of men seem to forget that the suffering in the world is not of His making. Why should He intervene? Have we either the merit or right to claim the manifestation of His goodwill rather than His wrath, as some deem calamities to be? Further, how would God intervene, seeing He endowed man with free agency and independent will, and man, alas, has used his God-given freedom in a way that has produced the suffering the world is afflicted with. To those of us who believe that He is a God at hand, and not afar off as a mere onlooker, we know that He is not powerless to achieve anything effective on behalf of man; that, since man in Eden introduced suffering to the world, He has intervened, especially at Calvary, when He dealt once and for all with the sin and consequent suffering of the world.

Many a godly soul suddenly overwhelmed by sorrow and loss is perplexed by God's apparent silence in response to their cry. Crushed by their suffering, theirs is the feeling expressed a century ago by Dean Mansel:

> There are times when the heaven that is over our heads seems to be brass, and the earth under us to be iron, and we feel our hearts sink within us under the calm pressure of unyielding and unsympathetic law.

We think of the way the earth drank in the blood of untold numbers of martyrs, the purest and noblest of men, and silent heaven looked down on their anguish as they were tortured to death. We readily admit that such evident silence has hardened some in unbelief. In his messianic psalm, David moaned:

> Reproach hath broken my heart; and I am full of heaviness: and I looked for some to take pity, but there was none; and for comforters, but I found none.
>
> 69:20

David's son Solomon, although in a world ruled and governed by a God he knew to be Almighty, sadly confessed:

> So I returned, and considered all the oppressions that are done under the sun: and behold the tears of such as were oppressed, and they had no comforter; and on the side

of their oppressors there was power; but they had no comforter.

Ecclesiastes 4:1

Jeremiah lamented, "though I call and cry for help, he shuts out my prayer" (Lamentations 3:8 RSV). Unrelieved suffering is brooded over, and too often, the cold mist of a settled unbelief quenches the last spark of faith. The heart is chilled by a sense of utter desolation, or, as in some cases, roused to rebellion by a sense of wrong. "Infidelity trades upon the silence of Heaven, the inaction of the Supreme." Are we not distinctly told that He neither slumbers nor sleeps (Psalms 121:3, 4)? Therefore, ever wide awake, and seeing the suffering of His own, why does He not act on their behalf?

Divine silence is evident in at least two Gospel incidents. The first is that of the Canaanite woman from Phoenicia (Matthew 15:21–28). Hearing of the Christ who went about doing good, she traveled a long way, and surmounted the stern, strong barrier of race to plead with a *Jew* about her very sick daughter. She felt that if only she could find Him, help would be forthcoming, amply rewarding her for the weight and weariness of her journey. When ultimately she stood before the great Healer, she challenged His perfect pity and power in a plea simple enough for an answer. The disciples, looking upon this brave, troubled mother, concerned only about her suffering child, besought Jesus to grant her request, and then, "send her away" (*see* Matthew 15:23). But He was silent, and did not deal with her plea on the instant, for we read, "He answered her not a word." At some time or other is this not the experience of many a pleading heart? Sometimes the silence that follows some request is not of moments, as with this mother's plea, but of years.

His silence, however, did not carry with it a refusal to comply with the loving mother's request for her demon-possessed, pain-stricken daughter, *and His silence did not silence her*. Worshiping the silent Healer, she answered Him when He broke the silence, to bring forth a wonderful commendation of her faith. Her beloved daughter was fully restored. She would not let Him go until He had blessed her. She was not perplexed by the strange silence of Jesus, but felt it to be a sympathetic silence. Somehow she saw in His face hope that helped her to remain for His reply. Had He not broken His silence, she would have returned with still deeper pain after having looked into the silent eyes of Eternal Love. But she went home grateful and happy, for He gave her not simply the best she asked for, but the best she was able to receive.

The other story concerns the sickness and death of Lazarus, whom Jesus loved (John 11:1–46). Martha and Mary, also loved by Jesus, sent Him a message that their brother was ill, knowing that He would understand and take immediate and appropriate action because of His affection for the family. Although receiving the urgent message, Jesus stayed where He was for two days. He took no quick action to heal Lazarus as He could have done by a word only, even at a distance. In fact, He said, "I am glad that I was not there" (*see* John 11:15). On the face of it, such a statement seems heartless, and as He tarried, and made no effort to hurry to the sick one, His friend worsened and died. When Jesus finally came to Bethany, Lazarus had been in his grave four days.

We can imagine how His delay and silence created a problem for Martha and Mary. Greatly troubled, Martha said to Jesus as He arrived at Bethany, "Lord, if Thou hadst been here, our brother would not have died." Answering He said, "Thy brother shall rise again." The dear sisters came to learn that His delay was not a denial, but a designed silence bringing greater glory to God and a most forcible illustration of His own miraculous power. Further, had it not been for that delay, we would not have had the most consoling phrase in the Bible for suffering hearts: *"Jesus wept,"* or better still, "Jesus shed tears." Also, a large number of souls would not have been saved (John 11:45; 12:11).

The lesson we learn from His silences and delays is that He is never before His time, or after. Because of His omniscience and omnipresence when the precise moment comes to act, He does so, decisively and beneficially, for He is a "very *present* help in trouble" (*see* Psalms 46:1). So, although He seems to tarry, we must wait, for He will surely come. "Our God shall come, and shall *not* keep silence . . ." (*see* Psalms 50:3). His seeming silence is not one of callous indifference or helpless weakness, but one which is a pledge of the utmost spiritual good for the sufferer. With a glorious end in view, the Lord does not spare from pain, but makes us perfect through the suffering endured. Through conflict a crown is won, and by the thorn track, we gain the city of quest. It was a storm, we are told, that led to the discovery of the gold mines of Hindustan. The psalmist could say, "Before I was afflicted I went astray: but now have I kept thy word" (119:67).

If one looks only upon his affliction and pain, his mind may become tortured with doubt; but if the sufferer is found "looking unto Jesus," he will find that the Hand inflicting the wound administers the balm. Faith, then, is necessary to trust Him where we cannot trace, and to follow Him even when we cannot fathom His purpose in delaying to come to our aid. "By the thorn road and no other is the mount of vision won." An unknown scholar in the School of Sympathy would have us remember:

> May Heaven ne'er trust my friend with happiness,
> Till it has taught him how to bear it well by previous pain.

4

Harmony Between Attributes and Action

We Rest in His Perfection

I do not know what next may come
  Across my pilgrim way;
I do not know tomorrow's road,
  Nor see beyond today.
But this I know—my Saviour knows
  The path I cannot see;
And I can trust His wounded hand
  To guide and care for me.

I do not know what may befall,
  Of sunshine or of rain,
I do not know what may be mine,
  Of pleasure and of pain;
But this I know—my Saviour knows,
  And whatsoe'er it be,
Still I can trust His love to give
  What will be best for me.

I do not know what may await,
  Or what the morrow brings:
But with the glad salute of faith,
  I hail its opening wings;
For this I know—that in my Lord
  Shall all my needs be met,
And I can trust the Heart of Him
  Who has not failed me yet.

E. MARGARET CLARKSON

I_F GOD KNOWS that His silence in suffering opposes His character, why does He not vindicate Himself and prove that as the Creator, nothing can outrun His control? His delay and inaction weaken the faith of many. When all around us is a world of woe and wickedness so adverse to His sovereignty, why does He not show His hand and demonstrate His power? Proudly we think how we would act if almighty. If He is the Good Samaritan to multitudes on the Jericho road of life, why does He not do something about the tragedies and sufferings of the travelers? He must know how His silence militates against Himself and all that He is presented to be. Why does He still maintain such silence?

The answer to such a pressing question is that He cannot act contrary to all He is in Himself.

> Yet if we are faithless he always remains faithful. He cannot deny his own nature.
>
> 2 Timothy 2:13 PHILLIPS

This implies that His *person* and His *practice* must be in perfect agreement. In a somewhat severe message to Timothy, Paul emphasizes that God cannot treat the faithless as though he were faithful, cannot act as though faithfulness and faithlessness were one and the same thing. In other words, He cannot go contrary to His own nature, or be guilty of double standards and partiality. What He does must be the reflection of all He *is*. Harmony must prevail between His attributes and actions—between character and conduct. Prominent among His virtues are His *love, wisdom,* and *justice,* and such must always characterize His dealings with men, whether, as sufferers, they are godly or ungodly. But the problem is to harmonize God's love and justice, particularly with the multiplied sufferings of a perfectly just person. That great epic, the Book of Job, shows that the one being arraigned before the bar of judgment is really not so much Job as *Jehovah,* who seemed to "multiply wounds *without cause*" (*see* 9:17).

GOD IS LOVE!

Love is the last and lasting revelation of the divine character. Ages before, His Word presented Him as Righteousness, Fountain of Life, Light, the Holy One. But it was given to John, the disciple whom Jesus loved, to give Him His new best name, and to declare not only that He is lovely or loving, but *is love*. Love is not only one of His glorious attributes but the texture of His very being. God *is* Love—the incarnation of unselfish benevolence that goes out to a lost world (*see* John 3:16). Therefore, in His dealings with His own who love Him, because He first loved them, He cannot be unloving in His treatment of them. When we are perplexed and troubled by our suffering, we err if we charge Him with being indifferent to our pain and anguish, or spiteful and vindictive. God is love, and because we are the objects and recipients of His love, we may safely trust ourselves to His providence—silent and mysterious though it seems to be. We must believe that if we love Him and are called according to His purpose, *all* things, even the most unwelcome experiences of life, are working together for our good (Romans 8:28). His is the love that will not let us go, and He chastens us that we may have the very best such love can bestow.

Every believer doing the will of the Father is the brother of Jesus (Matthew 12:50). He is not ashamed to call brethren all those redeemed by His precious Blood (Hebrews 2:11). If then He is the brother, His brotherly love must ever continue toward them. He will act kindly, and perform a brother's part. Such love, passing knowledge, forbids Him to be negligent, indifferent, or unconcerned of His brethren when they turn to Him in the hour of suffering. Manifesting toward them a brother's love, He will allay their fears, bear with their infirmities, meet their needs, console their hearts, and encourage their faith.

Jesus came as God's only-begotten and well-beloved Son and as the personification of His Father's love. Yet in spite of this most affectionate relationship, the Son was permitted to suffer as the Man of Sorrows. The bond binding Father and Son together was deeper than ours could ever be, yet in the darkest hour the Son never lost confidence in His Father's love. At the peak of His anguish He could still cry, *My God, My God!* Innocent, He yet submitted to all His Father allowed cruel men to do to Him. The Father did not intervene by sparing His Son from a cross of anguish and shame, but through it did something far better for Him. He made Jesus perfect through suffering, an example and comforter to all sufferers, and the Saviour of the world. In the continuing salvation of countless numbers of lost souls, He sees the travail of His soul and is satisfied.

GOD IS WISE!

The best of saints do not know what is best for them, because, at their best, they are fallible. It is not in them to direct their steps aright. "To err is human" because of the mind's involvement in original sin. But God is inconceivably wise, and all His ways are perfect. Having, therefore, infinite wisdom and knowledge, He cannot be ignorant of His children's trials and troubles, nor can He make a mistake or take a wrong turn in the ordering of their lives: "My son, suffer Me to do with thee what I please. I know what is expedient for thee."

As the "only wise God," He must ever act consistently with His own character, which forbids Him acting otherwise than planning the most beneficial results of permitted suffering. The psalmist could say, "I know, O Lord, that thy judgments are right, and that thou in faithfulness hast afflicted me" (119:75). His perfect wisdom prevents Him from willingly afflicting or grieving the children of men (Lamentations 3:33). Ignorant of the long-term blessings of what He allows us to endure, or in some trials He sends, we may deem Him unwise in the operation of His will. "What I do thou knowest not now; but thou shalt know hereafter" (John 13:7).

We must learn how to ask *wisdom* of God, who is ever ready to give wisdom. He is infinitely wise and invariably good in the molding of the characters of His own children. Always a sovereign, He performs His will whether in heaven or on earth, and none can dispute His right to accomplish His will in the wisest way. Thus, ours should be the attitude of constant surrender with the prayer, "Here am I. Do with me as seemeth *Thee* good." If He purposes to strip us, then it is for a deeper sanctity of life and to find our heaven in His company, grace, and offices. Because of His flawless wisdom, His charge of us and of our concerns will be to our greatest advantage.

In the midst of our suffering of heart or body, we

must not forget that He watches over us every moment of the day; that His omniscience enables Him to see what is best for us both now and in the future; that His omnipotence is engaged to defend us; and that His wisdom is constant to train and guide us. God is with us! The One whose love and wisdom we question is at our side, reading our thoughts and knowing us as no other. He silently pursues the beneficial end of the trial and sorrow He permits (Jeremiah 29:11). Our heavenly Father, who corrects us because He loves us, is too wise to err in His government of our lives, and too good to err through malice. Therefore, we can safely trust ourselves to His care, welcoming His discipline in suffering, confident that in so doing as He pleases, He will be pleased to do only what is the very best for us. As A. T. Pierson expresses it:

> It is in the deepest darkness of the starless midnight that men learn how to hold on to the hidden Hand most tightly and how that Hand holds them; that He sees where we do not, and knows the way He takes; and though the way be to us a roundabout way, it is the right way and leads to the city of habitation . . . .
>
> *Trial is the school of trust.* Faith gets new purity, temper, and tenacity in the furnace fires.

When I can trust my all with God,
  In trial's fearful hour,
Bow, all resign'd, beneath His rod,
  And bless His sparing power,
A joy springs up amidst distress,
A fountain in the wilderness.

GOD IS JUST!

As a just and righteous God, He cannot cause any child of His to suffer unnecessarily. His love, mercy, and wisdom never imperil His *justice*. Men may speak about the reticence of heaven as to the wrongs of earth, and of the withholding of punishment on those who cause His own children to suffer, but as the Judge of all the earth, He is ever consistent in such an office. Elisabeth Barrett Browning could write:

God's fruit of justice ripens slow:
Men's souls are narrow—let them grow!
My brother, we must wait!

If, because of our narrow outlook, God's justice ripens slow, inevitably it ripens for saint and sinner alike. Not only is He inconceivably wise, but inflexibly just. It was William Cowper who gave us the lines:

Know that the wrath Divine, when most severe,
Makes Justice still the guide of His career.
And will not punish in one mingled crowd,
Those without light, and thee without a cloud.

As for George Herbert, his tribute to divine justice is expressive:

Either grief will not come; or if it must
Do not forecast;
And while it cometh, it is almost past
Away, distrust!
My God hath promised, *He is just!*

Often mercy and justice are linked together. For instance, Anne Ross Cousin has taught us to sing:

With mercy and with judgment
My web of time He wove.

John Milton combines these two virtues in the verse:

In Mercy and Justice both,
Through heav'n and earth,—so shall My
glory excel;
But Mercy first and last shall brightest shine.

But in spite of these glowing tributes to mercy, it must be emphasized that God is merciful because, first of all, He is *just*. Does not the Apostle Paul tell us that God is just, and the justifier of all who believe (Romans 3:26)? Mercy toward the believing sinner springs from His perfect justice. As Frederick W. Faber puts it:

> Whom Justice makes All-Merciful,
> Omniscience makes All-Loving.

In His chastening through suffering, God is just in that He never applies more stripes than merited. All the pain and anguish of the cross became:

> Heaven's trysting place,
> Where Heaven's love and justice meet.
>
> ELIZABETH C. CLEPHANE

Justice demanded punishment for sin, and in His love God provided the One who should suffer death for every man. But His justice did not imperil His love and mercy. If a suffering heart is tempted to feel that God has not acted kindly or justly with him, let him remember Calvary.

5

Godliness Does Not Guarantee Immunity

Prayer of the Godly in Affliction

Father! that in the olive shade
  When the dark hour came on,
Didst, with a breath of heavenly air,
  Strenghten Thy Son:
Oh! by the anguish of that night,
  Send us down blessed relief:
Or to the chasten'd by Thy might
  Hallow this grief!
And Thou! that when the starry sky
  Saw the dread strife begun,
Didst teach adoring faith to cry,
  Thy will be done!
By Thy meek spirit, Thou of all
  That e'er have mourned the chief—
Thou, Saviour! if the strike must fall,
  Hallow this grief!

AUTHOR UNKNOWN

SCRIPTURE PLAINLY TEACHES that not all personal suffering is related to personal sin, even though all suffering is distantly related to sin. In the miracle of the healing of the man born blind (John 9), Jesus rejected the idea that personal or parental sin was responsible for such a physical calamity as congenital blindness. The disciples asked, "Who did sin, this man or his parents that he should be born blind?" The Master replied, "Neither this man sinned nor his parents" (*see* John 9:2, 3).

The haunting fear robbing many a heart of peace is that their suffering is the punishment of God for some form of sin in their life. A load of suffering fell on Job, as we shall presently see, yet, he ". . . was perfect and upright, and one that feared God, and eschewed evil" (Job 1:1). Crushed hopes, trials, sickness, and suffering, then, are not necessarily signs of God's anger, or of His punishment. Often the godliest suffer most because they are most able to bear their sorrow nobly.

Then there is the record about the Siloam tower disaster, and the supposition that this was the direct result of the sins of those who perished when the tower fell. Jesus did not assign any cause for the disaster in spite of His perfect knowledge of why it happened (Luke 13: 4, 5). Godly John the Baptist languished like some caged eagle in the fortress at Machaerus and suffered cruel martyrdom even though he was "a prophet of the Highest" (*see* Luke 1:75, 76). This finest and truest of the prophets, so just in life, was silenced by an unjust king. Holy forerunner though he was, God did not exempt him from terrible anguish.

Another aspect of the problem of suffering is the way many innocent people are made to endure it. We readily admit that we deserve some of the anguish we have to bear. We tell children that if they play with fire, they will get burned, and the Bible makes it clear that in the spiritual realm, obedience and joy go together, as do unbelief and impotence, sin and suffering. What we sow, whether in the flesh or the spirit, we inevitably reap. But the matter concerning us is that so much sorrow and pain come from the sin or thoughtlessness of others. War is a vast breeding ground of innocent human misery, as the terrible gas chambers of Belsen and Buchenwald in World War II so cruelly prove.

In the narrow world of our own personal life a surprising amount of inner grief and unhappiness is often caused by the thoughtlessness of those near to us, who become as a thorn in our flesh. Acquaintances, who are envious of our success and possessions, can make it unpleasant for us. Well we know what Paul did about the "thorn" that deeply disturbed his mind and peace. Three times he prayed for the removal of the cause of unmerited suffering, but the Lord answered by saying, ". . . My grace is sufficient for thee: for my strength is made perfect in weakness . . ." (2 Corinthians 12:9). So Paul continued bearing his "thorn" from Satan, because the Lord promised to bear him. Thus he came to "take pleasure" in all the severe trials he had to face. "When I am weak, then am I strong" (*see* 2 Corinthians 12:7–11).

Christians though we may be, we cannot expect to miss the sorrows of this life, for man is born to trouble as sparks fly upward. Sooner or later the legacy of suffering must be paid in installments, large or small. Suffering has no respect of persons. As God's sun shines impartially on the evil and the good, and His rain falls impartially on the just and the unjust, so pain overtakes, without discrimination, saint and sinner alike. Among the saints, the question is, how do we deal with our thorn? This is how an unknown poet expresses it:

Humbly I asked of God to give me joy,
To crown my life with blossoms of delight:
I begged for happiness without alloy,
Discovering that my pathway should be bright.

Prayerfully I sought these blessings to attain
And now I thank Him that He gave me pain,
For with my pain and sorrow came to me
A dower of tenderness in act and thought,
And with the suffering came a sympathy
And insight that success had never brought.
Father, I had been foolish and unblest
If Thou hadst granted me my blind request.

When trials and afflictions are permitted, we do well to ascertain if there is any reason why they are sent, or to learn the lessons they are meant to teach. We should also acknowledge the Lord's right to chasten, His love in doing so, and His wisdom in the time, nature, and duration of the trial. Also, by His grace, we should submit cheerfully, or at least silently, glorify Him in it, and after it, and be improved in our knowledge of Him, of sanctity and spirituality by all He permits.

God does not spare His children whom He calls "the apple of My eye" from trouble and calamities. What would happen to their characters if suffering overtook only the wicked? Certainly there are occasions when He does intervene and save His own from threatened calamity, but He does not spare them from any suffering whatever. If He did, then the Christian would turn out to be a cosmic pet. And a petted child is always a spoiled child. Some of the promises of the psalmist, however, would appear to be on the side of immunity of saints from disease and disaster:

> A thousand shall fall at thy side, and ten thousand at thy right hand; but it shall not come nigh thee. Only with thine eyes shalt thou behold and see the reward of the wicked . . . . There shall no evil befall thee, neither shall any plague come nigh thy dwelling . . . . With long life will I satisfy him . . . .
>
> Psalms 91:7, 8, 10, 16

While it is true that there were occasions when Israel appeared to have a charmed life, safe under divine protection, and saw the effect of perils pass by the nation harmlessly, yet these promises are not to be taken altogether literally. One knows of saints who succumbed when the plague of cancer came nigh their dwelling. Martyrs down the ages have experienced what it was to have evil befall them. As for those who love the Lord, and dwell in the secret place of the most high, it is not true that all of them are satisfied with long life. Robert Murray McCheyne, one of the godliest ministers Scotland has known, died at the early age of thirty.

What is the answer to the problem here? Well, E. Stanley Jones gives us a solution when he says:

If you spiritualize what the psalmist declares, it can be used; but if it is to be taken literally, then it raises questions. The New Testament does not teach this—nor does life teach it. It is the insistence upon the literal fulfillment of such promises as the above and the conflict it raises with the daily facts around one that stuns and shatters the faith of many. It simply does not work out that no plague comes nigh the dwelling of the righteous and that they are invariably satisfied with long life.

It is quite true that righteousness does tend to saner and healthier and longer living. A life lived in the Christian way fits the facts of the universe better, makes a man happier, and therefore on the whole gives longer life . . . . It raises more problems than it settles. In order to perfect His children in holiness, the refiner's fire is used, and forms of suffering prove preparatory, fitting them who are tried by fire for closer fellowship with God, a clearer revelation of Him, and a more effective service for Him. Some aspects of suffering are times of spiritual uplifting, like the dawn after a dark night of unbelief. The godliest, then, are not spared the action of "the Purifier of silver." Determined to perfect them, He casts His precious metal into His crucible. But all is well, for "Love is His thermometer, and marks the exact degree of heat; not one instant's unnecessary pang will He permit, and as soon as the dross is released so that He sees Himself reflected, the trial ceases."

That God's wise purpose be accomplished is of higher importance than our deliverance or immunity from suffering. Thus, a larger end is served than if we were left undisturbed, unruffled to enjoy life. The problem may be raised, why under the reign of a God of love should any child of His suffer? Why do the innocent suffer with the guilty? Why are the terrible agonies of the world, often involving some of God's choicest saints, permitted? It seems to us that a great deal of human misery is preventable. Much of it is the result of sin, and God must not be blamed for granting man free will. "Many cry over spilt milk when their proper business is to take measures which will protect the jug from being knocked over again."

Having already asked the question, "Why do the godly suffer?" perhaps we should give consideration to another question, namely, "Why shouldn't the godly suffer?" This may seem to be a provocative question, yet if God's beloved Son suffered so much, why should not those redeemed by His Blood suffer, seeing that perfection comes through suffering? If they do not suffer then how can they become "partakers of Christ's sufferings," as Peter expresses it (1 Peter 4:13)? Would-be disciples must be prepared to take up a cross—a cross representing submission to the will of God in suffering. Those who are branches of the Vine must accept the pruning knife if better and more abundant fruit in life and service is desired.

> Now the pruning, sharp, unsparing,
> Scattered blossom, bleeding shoot;
> Afterward, the plenteous bearing
> Of The Master's pleasant fruit.
>
> SARAH DOUDNEY

This was the way the Master went, and the godly must not shrink from following Him in His sorrow. Identification with Him includes the fellowship of His suffering.

Considering, more particularly, outstanding Bible saints who suffered, we have an enforced reason why the godly should suffer. Here are striking examples of how pain can produce gain, advantage can spring from affliction, and prosperity can come from adversity. Prominent among those of the Royal Order of Sufferers in the Old Testament is the patriarch Job who endured such mental and physical anguish that his wife urged him to end it all by cursing God and committing suicide. There were, of course, other well-known godly men, such as Joseph and Daniel, who underwent much trial in captivity, but lived to see their slavery turn to wonderful successes. Ultimately, the dark clouds, big with blessing, broke upon their heads.

Previously mentioned was Ezekiel who was not allowed by God to show any of the usual symptoms of human grief when his much-loved wife died. Surely there is no other story of sorrow quite like his. Yet God's hand was in His servant's anguish, as it is in ours. Prophet though he was, he knew deep, private sorrow, proving that no spiritual ministry can exempt one from the common lot of all men. In Ezekiel we see why the godly must suffer. It was divinely ordained for "Not a single shaft can hit—till the God of love sees fit." In the captive prophet, smitten with grief, we have a wonderful illustration of the transforming ministry of sorrow. Ezekiel became a channel of grace, and a sign of God's will to the people of his day.

THE SUFFERINGS OF JOB

Job was plagued as few men have been. In one fell swoop he lost all his material possessions, was crushed and pain-stricken by hateful boils covering his flesh, had a wife who was most unsympathetic, and professed comforters who were useless in his dark hour of trial. What "an example of suffering affliction" Job is! (*See* James 5:10, 11.) What an object lesson in patience and faith he was before God, his family, friends, and foes. It was from his lips during his sore affliction that he gave utterance to some of the most sublime of all words in Scripture. Think of these:

> Though he slay me, yet will I trust in him . . . .
>
> 13:15

> . . . when he hath tried me, I shall come forth as gold.
>
> 23:10

> For I know that my redeemer liveth, and that he shall stand at the latter day upon the earth: And though after my skin worms destroy this body, yet in my flesh shall I see God: Whom I shall see for myself, and mine eyes shall behold, and not another; though my reins be consumed within me.
>
> 19:25–27

Job portrays why the godly should suffer. It is because trial is a trust from the Giver of every good and perfect gift to be borne for His glory. The severe testing of Job opens with his being delivered over to Satan to be tried, and after the stripping the patriarch received, it ends with his possessing twice as much as he had had before. The temptation of Jesus, as we shall presently see, opens with His conflict with the three subtle temptations of the same satanic foe and ends with His emerging from His trial full of the power of the Spirit. We ask again, "Why *shouldn't* the godly suffer?" when we see that the end of conflict is character heightened in its spiritual perceptions and deepened in its capacity to share with others. In both cases, evil turned to good because the tried one believed that evil as well as good should be received from the hand of God.

With his boil-covered body and ensuing pain and discomfort, Job must have had many a sleepless night. Yet he did not sigh, but sing. God gave His servant songs in the night, and he did not sin with his lips. Sleeplessness is common to many who are burdened with physical or mental suffering, but if it be God's will, who giveth sleep, to withhold it as He did with King Ahasuerus, then it is for His glory and the benefit of others. "That night the king could not sleep." But who can doubt that that sleepless night was not designed by God when it spared the whole Jewish nation from wholesale slaughter (*see* Esther 6:1; 3:6)? What then is the message of suffering Job? Let Dr. John R. Stott give the satisfying answer:

> When faced with calamity or stricken with sickness, the mind must not be engrossed in our sickness (for that is morbid self-pity), nor

in our sins (for that is introspective self-accusation), but partly in the moral and spiritual profit to be derived from suffering, which is valuable self-discipline, and best of all in God Himself. This is humble self-surrender to the God of power and wisdom and love, Who has been fully and finally revealed in the Cross. This is the sober, wise realism of Christian worship.

THE SUFFERINGS OF JESUS

Coming to the New Testament we have in the recorded miracles various aspects of suffering, how they were dealt with, and how they were made to magnify God's grace and power in the lives of those afflicted. It should be carefully noticed that there are examples of those who endured unrelieved physical pain yet were recognized as saintly in life. For instance, we have Paul's three friends: Epaphroditus, "sick unto death, not regarding his life" (*see* Philippians 2:25–30); Trophimus, "left at Miletum sick" (*see* 2 Timothy 4:20); and Timothy, for whose "stomach's sake and often infirmities" (*see* 1 Timothy 5:23) Paul prescribed, not more faith, but medicinal treatment.

But most prominent as sufferers are the Lord Jesus and Paul. First, then, let us consider Jesus who, although the Son of God, suffered many things, and who:

> In every pang that rends the heart
> As the Man of Sorrows has a part.
>
> MICHAEL BRUCE

It is because He was tried and tested in all points as we are that He was touched with the feeling of our infirmities. This is why we can best interpret our own sufferings and those of others in the light of all that He endured.

At the head of the procession of the world's sufferers is a thorn-crowned Man, the revelation of sacrificial love for others, "His pain healing our pains, His wounds answering our wounds, His love taking our sins . . . The crown of life is man, the crown of man is Christ, the crown of Christ is the cross." The Christ who had never known suffering would not be the Christ for broken hearts. We might well ask ourselves, "Which would you choose of the two Christs who were equal in every other way, except that the one had never known any suffering while the other had lived intimately with it?" Would not our immediate answer be that the Christ we call Saviour would be far short of that which He is to us if He had been a stranger to suffering, travail, and sorrow? Did He not say of His personal anguish, ". . . see if there be any sorrow like unto my sorrow . . ." (Lamentations 1:12)? With such a pattern before us, do we yet shun the discipline of suffering, that which makes our life more Christlike?

What were the sufferings of Christ?

He knew poverty. He was born in a stable. As the carpenter of Nazareth He had to work long and hard. In His ministry among men He had nowhere to lay His head, and when He died, He had nothing to leave for others to divide but His seamless robe.

He knew loneliness. "Jesus was found alone." A felt solitariness was His. ". . . the disciples forsook him and fled" (Matthew 26:56). And in the blackest hour of all, His own heavenly Father turned away from Him. He died alone, totally alone, for our sins.

He knew fatigue. One day He was so tired He slept in a small boat during a storm. Then there was the occasion when "wearied with His journey," He rested on the curbing of Jacob's well.

He knew hunger. During the time of His temptation, He knew well the gnawing pangs of physical need. In another season, as He approached Bethany, the Lord again experienced hunger and searched in vain for a piece of fruit among the leaves of a fig tree.

He knew thirst. He expressed it to the woman at the well and to His tormentors at the foot of the cross.

He knew ill treatment and unbelief of family and friends. Friends said He was "beside Himself," or out of His mind. His own brothers did not believe in Him and His chosen disciples were slow of heart to believe. ". . . his own received him not" (John 1:11).

He knew pain. He anticipated it, and yet steadily

set His face to meet it. He suffered the most terrible kind of actual mental and physical pain when He was scourged, crowned with thorns, and nailed to a tree.

> But none of the ransomed ever knew
> How deep were the waters crossed;
> Or how dark was the night that the Lord
> passed through,
> Ere He found His sheep that was lost.
>
> "The Ninety and Nine"
> ELIZABETH C. CLEPHANE

Having experienced all these trials as a Man on earth, now as the glorified Lord, He can sympathize and strengthen all His own in their suffering (Hebrews 2:17, 18; 4:14–16). It was way back in the third century that Gregory of Nazianzus gave the following vivid picture of the contrasts between the life of Christ and the church:

> Christ hungered as man, and fed the hungry as God. He was hungry as man, and yet He is the Bread of Life; He was athirst as man, and yet He says, "Let him that is athirst come unto me and drink"; He was weary, and yet He is our rest; He pays tribute, and yet He is a King; He is called a devil, and yet casts out devils. He prays, and yet hears prayer; He weeps, and dries our tears; He is sold for

thirty pieces of silver, and redeems the world. He is "led as a sheep to the slaughter," and is the Good Shepherd; He is mute like a sheep, and yet He is the Everlasting Word; He is the "man of sorrows," but He heals our pains; He is nailed to a Tree and dies upon it, and by the Tree restores us to life; He has vinegar to drink, and changes the water into wine; He lays down His life, and takes it again; He dies, and gives life, and by dying destroys death.

Job held the field in suffering until a Greater came. The afflicted man of Uz was the forerunner of the Man, Jesus of Nazareth, over whom all the waves and billows of affliction passed, and yet He died in faith. He felt, as no other, the pain of a lost, guilty world. That weight of human guilt finally broke His heart. Yet as He hanged upon a cross of shame, His enemies, with keen eyes of hatred, scrutinized the purposes of His brief ministry and dragged into prominence two characteristics which, more than any other, marked His service among men. They cried tauntingly: "He saved others"; "He trusted in God." But as Faber wrote of these two sayings, "Strange that such wicked words should be so beautiful; yet, are they not as beautiful, because they are true?" May the same be true of you and me! Having trusted in God, and dying for others, He alone can save them.

Jehovah bade His sword awake,
  O Christ, it woke 'gainst Thee!
Thy blood the flaming blade must slake;
  Thy heart its sheath must be—
All for my sake, my peace to make;
  Now sleeps that sword for me.

ANNE ROSS COUSIN

THE SUFFERINGS OF PAUL

It would seem as if the renowned Apostle to the Gentiles knew more than most men of his time—that the dark threads were needful in the Weaver's skillful hands. A whole skein of such threads were woven into his life for Christ's sake, and for others. His was the inner knowledge and the deep, prolonged experience of "the fellowship of His sufferings." He wrote in 2 Corinthians 6:10: ". . . having nothing, and yet possessing all things." Paul exulted even in his persecutions and trials.

In those days rich and poor alike went to school, then on to learn a trade. Paul became a tent maker, and during the time he mentions when he had to repair tents to keep body and soul together, such close work must have been a strain on his sore eyes. Evidently he suffered from some severe eye trouble, causing the saints in the church at Galatia much concern about this defect. This led Paul to write in gratitude: ". . . I bear you record, that, if it had been possible, ye would have plucked out your own eyes, and have given them to me" (Galatians 4:15). He concluded his epistle by referring to the large lettering he was forced to use in writing to them (*see* Galatians 6:11).

After meeting the glorified Christ on the Damascus road, the former Saul of Tarsus was given the following commission by Ananias:

> . . . he is a chosen vessel unto me, to bear
> my name before the Gentiles, and kings, and
> the children of Israel: *For I will shew him how
> great things he must suffer* for my name's sake.
>
> Acts 9:15, 16, italics added

While the Book of Acts reveals how Paul did suffer, his own summary of trials he endured for Christ's sake makes gruesome reading:

> . . . in labours more abundant,
> in stripes above measure,
> in prisons more frequent,
> in deaths oft.
> Of the Jews five times received I forty stripes
>   save one.
> Thrice was I beaten with rods,
> once was I stoned,
> thrice I suffered shipwreck,

a night and a day I have been in the deep;
In journeyings often,
in perils of waters,
in perils of robbers,
in perils by mine own countrymen,
in perils by the heathen,
in perils in the city,
in perils in the wilderness,
in perils in the sea,
in perils among false brethren;
In weariness and painfulness,
in watchings often,
in hunger and thirst,
in fastings often,
in cold and nakedness.
Beside those things that are without, that
   which cometh upon me daily, the care of
   all the churches.

                    2 Corinthians 11:23–28

What an amazing, incomparable record! What a life of suffering without murmuring but with a heart exalting God. Listen to him as he says, "If I must needs glory, I will glory of the things which concern mine infirmities" (2 Corinthians 11:30). He never grumbled over his severe trials but made a boast of them. Instead of complaining at his persecutions, he learned to take pleasure in them—not vainly nor morbidly but "for Christ's sake," who had called him to suffer the loss of all things. As he reviewed his extreme privations and trials, he described them as "light affliction, which is for a moment, working for us more and more exceedingly an eternal weight of glory" (*see* 2 Corinthians 4:17, 18). The remarkable Apostle found that he could not experience spiritual maturity except through the suffering under which he was patient and submissive to the will of God. Others among the apostles grievously suffered for Christ's sake, such as saintly John. [For coverage of all they endured, the reader is referred to the author's volume *All the Apostles of the Bible.*]

> They climbed the steep ascent of heaven
> Through peril, toil, and pain:
> O God, to us may grace be given
> To follow in their train.
> "The Son of God Goes Forth to War"
> HENRY S. CUTLER

A wit remarked that far too many easy-going Christians prefer to follow the martyrs of old *in a train.*

6

How to Meet Suffering

Others

Lord, help me live from day to day
 In such a self-forgetful way
That even when I kneel to pray
 My prayers will be for Others.

Help me in all the work I do
 To ever be sincere and true
And know that all I do for You
 Must needs be done for Others.

Let Self be crucified and slain
 And buried deep, and all in vain
May efforts be to rise again
 Unless to live for Others.

And when my work on earth is done
 And my new work in heaven begun
May I forget the crown I've won
 While thinking still of Others.

Others, Lord, yes, Others
 Let this my motto be;
Help me to live for Others
 That I may live like Thee.

CHARLES D. MEIGS

Suffering, we find, has several hues—all evident at Calvary. We see *lawful suffering* exhibited in the two thieves on their crosses. Here we have the relationship between the cause and the effect—penalty following wrongdoing. This is the easiest kind of suffering to understand, having no air of mystery about it.

Then there is *compelled suffering,* seen in the way Simon, the Cyrenian, was forced to bear a cross though he did not deserve it. He happened to be on the scene when there was a need, and was conscripted to bear the load. History is replete with gruesome illustrations of this aspect of suffering. We also have *shared suffering*—the little group at the foot of the cross, Mary the mother of Jesus, and John His much-loved disciple. There is no doubt they shared the sorrow of the Man of Sorrows Himself. Both of them had shared joy in the One they loved, but they could not share the joy without sharing the pain. How their presence must have consoled the heart of the crucified One.

But the most noble form of suffering is *chosen*

suffering, not lawful, compelled, nor shared, but something infinitely deeper. Jesus could have come down from the cross and saved Himself, but He remained upon it until He cried, "It is finished!" His life was not taken by cruel men, but given voluntarily. "I lay down my life."

Do not these forms of suffering still operate? Many suffer because they merit it. They live in a lawful world, in which its laws cannot be violated without pain. Others, particularly in atheistically controlled countries, experience compelled suffering; and parents know what shared suffering is because of the loving bond of the home. Too few of us emulate the example of chosen suffering the cross presents. Paul, John, Peter and others of the early church knew what it was to take their share of suffering for the Gospel, because they did not live before a mirror, but looked out of a window upon a lost world. Those who live by sharing know what the unknown poet meant when he wrote "Pain":

The cry of man's anguish went up to God,
"Lord, take away my pain! . . ."
Then answered the Lord to the cry of the world,
"Shall I take away pain,
And with it the power of the soul to endure,
Made strong by the strain?
Shall I take away pity that knits heart to heart,
And sacrifice high?

Will ye lose all your heroes that lift from the fire
White brows to the sky?
Shall I take away love that redeems with a price,
And smiles with its loss?
Can ye spare from your lives that would cling unto
     mine
The Christ of His Cross?"

Our difficulty, however, is not so much with the enigma or with specific manifestations of suffering, but how to meet it, no matter in what guise it may come to us. Heathenism, and various religious systems, have different methods of facing pain, sorrow, and calamity—many of them stoical in nature. Attitudes determine our actions, for good or bad. Therefore it is of paramount importance to know how to cultivate the right outlook. As Edmund Vance Cooke puts it:

Oh, a trouble's a ton, or a trouble's an ounce,
    Or a trouble is what you make it,
And it isn't the fact that you're hurt that counts,
    But only how did you take it?

E. Stanley Jones refers to an Indian tribe in South America that begins early to instill into its young the attitude of inwardly steeling oneself against suffering. As soon as a child is born, the father greets it with these words, "You are born into a world of trouble. Shut your mouth, be quiet, and bear it." Such a stoical position is the product of this early hardening. But do not many in our so-called Christian country adopt the same sentiment when they harden themselves inwardly against the trials and sorrows overtaking them? Abigail Cresson captures this determined spirit in her expressive poem:

> Though I am beaten
> Nobody shall know.
> I'll wear defeat proudly;
> I shall go
> About my business
> As I did before.
> Only when I have safely
> Closed the door
> Against friends and the rest
> Shall I be free
> To bow my head
> Where there is none to see.
> Tonight I will shed my tears;
> Tomorrow when
> I talk with you
> I will be gay again.
> Though I am beaten
> Nobody shall guess,
> For I will walk
> As though I knew success.

Jesus, who accepted the fact of human suffering but did not explain it, or try to explain it away, urged disciples to take positive action in dealing with sorrow and trial. Describing the persecutions and prisons His followers would have to face, He said that their attitude toward them should be that of using them for the highest ends. "They shall turn unto you for a testimony," or, as it can be translated, "They shall turn out for you as an opportunity for witnessing" (*see* Luke 21:12, 13). Calamities were to be turned into confession, trials into testimony of divine grace. They would not escape trouble, nor merely bear it as the will of God. They must *use it,* making it contribute to magnificent ends. "Jesus implies that the Christian has learned the secret of an alchemy by which the base metal of injustice and consequent suffering can be turned into the gold of character and into the gold of the purposes of the kingdom of God."

The Master could emphasize this way of meeting suffering, for it was His own persistent attitude. We read that He *bore* His cross, but He did more than bear it, and allow it to bear Him—*He used it.* When we think of the betrayal by Judas, the mock trial, and then the cruel cross, surely no man ever endured such terrible injustice, yet He turned it all into a healing of injustice and sin. At the cross, men revealed themselves at their worst, but through His travail, Jesus revealed God at His best. At Calvary: "Hate was bitterest and there Love met it, and conquered it by taking it into His own heart and transforming it. The darkest hour of history becomes the lightest! The cross becomes a throne! The end—a new beginning."

John Milton wrote the phrase, "Can suffer, best can do."

Afflictions, which are chastisements, are sent in love. Let us not be afraid of the term *chastisement*. The original meaning of *chastise* is "to bring up or rear a child, to train, to instruct, educate, correct"—hence, the Greek proverb, "To learn is to suffer." The term has also the implication of "nourishment," or something good for us. This is why we are not to despise it, nor faint under it (*see* Hebrews 12:5). But we do despise the chastening of the Lord if we think we would be better without it, or when we brood over why it was sent, or when we adopt a carnal, flesh-pleasing attitude to be delivered from it as quickly as possible.

If we are sincere scholars in the school of suffering, affliction makes for enrichment of Christian character, and out of such we are taught true values and the right order of priorities. Adversity arranges the assets of our balance sheet in accordance with the perfect accountancy of heaven. Paul knew a great deal about this heavenly accountancy when he suffered the loss of all things, counting them as dung in comparison with gaining Christ. To summarize then, it would seem as if there are several ways by which we can meet pain and sorrow.

The stoic attitude of the Indian tribe just mentioned illustrates the resignation approach. It is a grin-and-bear facing of suffering. This comes when we use suffering as a mirror, and not as a window. We refuse to see the possible good of what God permits and whine in self-pity, or complain angrily of God's heartlessness or unconcern. Life is full of heroes in this class who endure their trials with remarkable fortitude. Robert Southey in his *Curse of Kehama* describes this class:

> The virtuous heart and resolute mind are free,
> Thus in their wisdom did the Gods decree
> When they created man. Let come what will
> This is one rock of strength; In every ill,
> Sorrow, oppression, pain and agony,
> The spirit of the good is unsubdued,
> And suffer, as they may, they triumph still.

All who have learned from Jesus through His redemption the secret of using suffering to bring life and healing to others are those who have discovered that a window is better than a mirror.

Reading the Warrick Lectures on Preaching, given by Dr. A. John Gossip in 1925 to theological students in Edinburgh, and preserved in his volume

In Christ's Stead, we came across this illustration which seems apt at this point:

> A wise servant being asked, "And which is Wordsworth's study?" opened a door. "This is his library," she said, "but his study is outside."

And ours must be there too, if we are ever to be preachers. Anatole France speaks of " 'bookish souls for whom the Universe is but paper and ink.'. The man whose body is animated by such a soul spends his life before his desk, without any care for the realities whose graphic representation he studies so obstinately. *He has never looked out of the window* . . . . At all events the world feels that we don't know men, that we shut ourselves into a cramped little corner; that we never looked out of the window."

No man is able to define the mystery of the cross, but countless millions have experienced what it is to be saved from the penalty and power of sin as the result of all the Saviour endured. Those who live near Him offer their hurt and grief along with His. Their sufferings bravely borne, although they may never know it, have inspired and encouraged others around. These saintly hearts proudly share in Christ's saving work, and He gladly and greatly uses them and their wonderful endurance for His Kingdom and His glory.

7

Beside the Waters of Comfort

Eternal Goodness

I know not what the future hath
Of marvel or surprise,
Assured alone that life and death,
His mercy underlies.

And so beside the Silent Sea
I wait the muffled oar;
No harm from Him can come to me
On ocean or on shore.

I know not where His islands lift
Their fronded palms in air;
I only know I cannot drift
Beyond His love and care.

And Thou, O Lord, by whom are seen
Thy creatures as they be,
Forgive me if too close I lean
My human heart on Thee.

JOHN GREENLEAF WHITTIER

THE Book of Common Prayer translates "He leadeth me beside the still waters" as "He shall . . . lead me forth beside the waters of comfort" (*see* Psalms 23:1). And in this chapter we shall rest beside these waters for little. Shakespeare wrote the phrase, "Love comforteth, like sunshine after rain." Such loving, refreshing consolation can alone come from Him who is the God of *all* comfort, willing to comfort us in our tribulation. Our consolation abounds in Him (2 Corinthians 1:3–7). When the cradle is emptied; when the young wife and mother, the husband and father, are stricken down; when friends deceive and betray us; when sickness, disease, or accident befall us; when reverses come through no fault of our own, and it is a grim struggle to make ends meet; when buoyant hopes are crushed; when we reach the end of the road with a body riddled with pain and weariness—to whom can we go for consolation but to Him who cried:

> Comfort ye! Comfort ye my people! Speak comfortably unto them!
>
> *See* Isaiah 40:1, 2

Down through the ages saints faced dark experiences, many of them being stripped of all they possessed, yet they proved that there was a love comforting them like sunshine after rain. They had a Friend by their side who had promised never to leave them, and thus were able to say with the poet: "Take from me everything Thou wilt, But go not Thou away." These valiant hearts did not faint in the day of adversity but gathered strength and courage from the comfort of the Scriptures. When the darkness was dense, they would speak to themselves the consoling words, "Why art thou cast down, O my soul? . . . *hope thou in God* . . ." (Psalms 42:5, 11 italics added). Today, so heavy with suffering, grief, pain, and disaster, there is not a person who does not need comfort at some time or another. If we are called to console them in their hour of stress and sorrow, we cannot do so unless first of all we ourselves know what it is to be comforted of God. A saying of Virgil reads:"There are tears in the affairs of this life, and human sufferings touch the hearts." But our hearts are not touched by human sufferings unless they have been touched by God's chastening rod.

Job called his three friends, who had come to console with him in his hour of extreme grief, "miserable comforters," and they deserved such an epithet because they asked Job not to think of his suffering but his sin. Theirs was the philosophy that all sickness and calamity were the fruit of sin—the inevitability of cause and effect. Without doubt much suffering is due to sin, if not our own, than others. But the dramatic Book of Job declares that the patriarch's sufferings were not a token of God's judgment upon him for wickedness; they were rather an evidence of God's confidence in him for his integrity. Elihu was a different kind of a comforter as we can gather from his magnificent description of the purpose of God's chastening (Job 33:14–30). The world could do with more comforters of his kind!

The celebrated Dr. Moon, inventer of the Moon System of reading for the blind, said, "God gave me blindness as a talent to be used in His service, that I might see the needs of those who could not see." He became a comforter to an innumerable company of sightless men and women because he believed that his similar affliction was a gift from above (John 19:11). To all in this world of woe with its sorrow and suffering, troubles and trials, there are five sources of consolation for sad hearts: the comfort of God, the comfort of Christ, the comfort of the Spirit, the comfort of Scripture, and the comfort of other saints.

THE COMFORT OF GOD

Paul rightly calls Him "The God of all comfort" (*see* 2 Corinthians 1:3, 4), for as the Creator and Father, He knows how best to comfort grief-stricken hearts in all their tribulations. He calls Himself "the God of all comfort" because He is ready to comfort at all times, and also because He is all-sufficient and thus able to meet every possible need that may arise. "God comforteth those that are cast down" (*see* 2 Corinthians 7:6). Is He not "the Father of mercies," therefore the One who has compassion on His children? If, then, we "joy in God" (*see* Romans 5:11), our hearts have a source of continual comfort. If we joy in friends, they die; if we joy in moods and feelings, they change; if we joy in possessions, they take wings and fly away; but if we joy in God, though the exercise of joy may be interrupted by suffering, the Object remains eternally the same. Even through our trials we rejoice evermore because we believe that He knows best.

> His love in times past, forbids me to think
> He'll leave me at last, In trouble to sink;
> Each sweet Ebenezer I have in review
> Confirms His good pleasure to help me quite
>   through.

Brother Lawrence has taught us how to "practice the presence of God," and to be able to do this is an unfailing source of comfort.

All my springs, O Lord, are in Thee,
Comforts for all the trials that be;
Consolation for sorrow's dark hour,
Strength that saves from Satan's power.

That fascinating character of a past generation, Billy Bray, the Cornish miner, experienced much of God's comfort amid his many trials. He said that if his persecutors shut him up in a barrel that he would shout *Glory!* through the bunghole. Billy had joy and comfort in spite of what happened for his happiness was not dependent upon happenings, but "in spite of" them. As we know, he named one of his feet *Glory* and the other *Hallelujah* so that when he walked, one of them said *Glory* and the other replied *Hallelujah.* It was said of him, "It was a sure instinct for Billy to name his feet, and not the roads, for some of the roads might lead to gardens and some might lead into gloom, but with him the feet still sounded their message, no matter what the road."

THE COMFORT OF CHRIST

Being one with His Father, Jesus shared His attribute of comfort, and so Paul could write to the church at Thessalonica, "Our Lord Jesus Christ himself . . . hath given us everlasting consolation and good hope through grace, *Comfort* your hearts . . ." (2 Thessalonians 2:16, 17 italics added). While among men, He was moved with deep compassion as He saw the souls around Him as sheep having no shepherd. The Gospels portray Him as a marvelous Comforter, untiring in His efforts to ease the burdens of others. When He saw tears, He dried them; when He met sickness and disease He banished them; when His own were fearful, He calmed their troubled hearts as He cried to the troubled sea, "Peace, be still!" When He came face to face with repentant sinners, He transformed their lives; when He encountered hungry multitudes, He fed them; when He passed a funeral procession, He broke it up and raised the corpse being carried to the grave. What an unfailing Comforter He was, and will ever be, seeing His consolation is everlasting in nature.

The consolations of Christ certainly abounded for that courageous Lutheran Pastor, Benjamin Schmolck, whose story A. T. Pierson relates. First of all he suffered from a fire that devastated his parents; then from a bereavement that emptied his home; then from a paralysis that left him a blind and helpless cripple. Yet out of his tribulation came a hymn of true beauty which can only be understood in the light of his adversity. On his bed, after his accumulated afflictions, he dictated the following verses:

My Jesus, as Thou wilt;
  Oh, may Thy will be mine!
Into Thy hand of love
  I would my all resign.
Through sorrow or through joy
  Conduct me Thine own
And help me still to say,
  My Lord, Thy will be done.

My Jesus, as Thou wilt.
  Though seen through many a tear,
Let not my star of hope
  Grow dim or disappear.
Since Thou on earth hast wept
  And sorrowed oft alone,
If I must weep with Thee,
  My Lord, Thy will be done.

My Jesus, as Thou wilt.
  All shall be well for me;
Each changing future scene
  I gladly trust with Thee.
Thus to my home above
  I travel calmly on
And sing, in life or death,
  My Lord, Thy will be done.

THE COMFORT OF THE SPIRIT

Before Jesus left the earth as the Comforter, He promised to send another in His place to console the distressed even as He had done. He could not leave them comfortless. Hence, the promise, "The Father [God of all comfort] shall give you another Comforter . . . the Holy Spirit" (*see* John 14:16, 26). The word *another* has a two-fold implication—another of the *same* kind, or another of a *different* kind. The Greek word Jesus used of the Spirit was the first: another of the *same* kind—"another like Myself." Thus, the ministry of consolation is continued by the Spirit. As for the term *Comforter,* it means "one called alongside to help." Jesus was the visible Comforter on earth. The Holy Spirit is the believer's invisible, indwelling Comforter, sent to help his ignorance and infirmities and to make intercession (Romans 8:26, 27).

When Paul returned to his own city of Tarsus, he was encouraged as he found the saints "walking in the comfort of the Holy Spirit" and consequently was blessed in the winning of souls (*see* Acts 9:31). Like Christ, the consolation of the Spirit was a "comfort of love" (*see* Philippians 2:1), and seen also in the "fruit of the Spirit" (*see* Galatians 5:22, 23). In days of trouble and affliction as in days of rest and prosperity, those early saints had recourse to a divine source of comfort.

As He is the Spirit of grace and supplication, we are dependent upon His unutterable intercession for us. We are so weak that none but He can enable us to pray with fervor, faith, and success, making us more than conquerors in our suffering.

Whatever your particular trial or suffering may be at this time, may the Lord grant you the experience of being "replenished with the consolation of the Holy Spirit," as the Rhenish version translates Acts 9:31. The Spirit is God *in* us, hence His ability to undertake for every one of us.

THE COMFORT OF SCRIPTURE

In his Letter to the Romans, Paul emphasizes that all that was written in the Old Testament was ". . . written for our learning, that we through patience and comfort of the scriptures might have hope" (Romans 15:4). Thus we have not only the comfort of the Trinity, but also the comfort of the Word which the Trinity inspired. The world does not possess another book of consolation comparable to the Bible.

The story is told of a lady of wealth who consulted her physician as to her state of health, but he could find nothing wrong with her except her extreme nervousness and irritability. She was highly incensed, however, when the only prescription he gave her was, "Go home and read the Bible a great deal and pray often, and come back in a month and report your condition." He insisted most kindly that it was the only course he could advise.

The lady returned home and began reading and praying, and after a month she was fully restored and visited her doctor again to report the success of his spiritual suggestion. She learned "the comfort of the Scriptures" in daily life and experience. Too many Christians suffer from spiritual starvation because of the lack of spiritual food daily feasting on Scripture provides. Its promises and precepts "make wise the simple," "rejoice the heart," and "enlighten the eyes" because they are "perfect" (*see* Psalms 19:7–11).

Comfort from "the God of all comfort" comes to us through "the comfort of the Scriptures" in the time of need, of suffering, of loss and distress. Old Testament promises and prophecies were of great comfort to Jesus while on earth suffering many things. Hence His repeated, *"It is written!"* Here are some Scriptures enabling us to derive comfort, to know His will, and to be lovingly submitted to Him:

If you are discouraged, read Isaiah 40.
If you are in doubt, or lack faith, read Hebrews 11, 12.
If you are weary of those who oppose you, read Psalms 37:1–7.

If you fear spiritual conflict and the fight is hard, read Psalm 27.

If you feel your lack of spiritual desires, read Romans 8.

If your love for others or for God is weak, read 1 Corinthians 13.

If you lack a knowledge of God's Law, read Exodus 20; Matthew 22:34–40.

If you find it hard to forgive, or to seek forgiveness, read Psalms 32:51; Matthew 18.

If you do not have eternal life, read John 3:1–18.

If you are afraid to die, read John 14:1–18.

If you desire a vision of heaven, read Revelation 21, 22.

THE MUTUAL COMFORT AMONG SAINTS

It is Paul, the apostle of consolation, who gave us the delightful exhortation, *"Comfort one another"* (*see* 1 Thessalonians 4:18; 2 Corinthians 2:1–4). But we can only experience this mutual comfort as, personally, each believer is comforted by God through the Scriptures. The lack of that warm, heartening, and consoling fellowship among many believers today is because of the lack of the everlasting consolation of Jesus within each heart. When every believer walks in the comfort of the Holy Spirit what else can they do but comfort one another when they meet?

The heart that has not suffered has little comfort to give to those who weep and suffer in a sorrowing world, because sympathy is born of experience. We are only capable of comforting one another, when, individually, we know the joy of divine comfort. We can picture Beethoven fighting his increasing deafness and all the time pouring out great streams of sublime music. We cannot know whether he himself heard his great music in spite of his deafness or because of it. But we do know that in producing his musical masterpieces when thus afflicted, he left remarkable music that has charmed the world ever since.

The most precious fruit in the fellowship of believers is the result of personal sorrow and suffering. Paul endured many tribulations, and left us the two important lessons he learned from such, namely, the way God can comfort us in all our trials and anguish, and how He can prepare us with like solace to comfort one another (2 Corinthians 1:4, 5). Paul, however, makes it clear that the way saints are to comfort one another is by words—words backed by God's own character, loving purpose, and power.

What a power there is in words for good or evil! This is why we are urged to set a watch upon our lips, because:

Words are little things of little cost,
quickly spoken, quickly lost.
Oh! how often ours have been idle words
and words of sin!
We forget them, but they stand witnesses
at God's right hand.

JOHN GEORGE FLEET

The apostle urged the saints at Thessalonica to "comfort one another with *these* words," referring to the Lord's glorious appearing in the air to gather all His redeemed children together, so that they could ever be with Him (*see* 1 Thessalonians 4:15–18). What comfort there is in these wonderful words, for when He returns, our sorrows will all be over, and we shall be forever removed from the bondage of our suffering flesh. Surely no words can comfort our hearts like those assuring us that we shall no more be separated from the Lord or from one another forever.

8

Where Eyes Are Never Wet With Tears

Some Time
We'll Understand

Not now, but in the coming years,
　　It may be in the better land,
We'll read the meaning of our tears,
　　And there, some time, we'll understand.

We'll catch the broken thread again,
　　And finish what we here began;
Heav'n will the mysteries explain,
　　And then, ah, then, we'll understand.

We'll know why clouds instead of sun
　　Were over many a cherished plan;
Why song has ceased when scarce begun;
　　'Tis there, some time, we'll understand.

God knows the way, He holds the key,
　　He guides us with unerring hand;
Sometime with tearless eyes we'll see;
　　Yes, there, up there, we'll understand.

Then trust in God through all thy days;
　　Fear not, for He doth hold thy hand.
Though dark thy way, still sing and praise,
　　Some time, some time, we'll understand.

MAXWELL N. CORNELIUS

At present, God has a bottle for our tears (Psalms 56:8), to catch every tear falling from the eyes of His suffering saints. Matthew Henry's rich commentary of the psalmist's lovely symbol reads:

> God has a bottle and a book for his people's tears, both those for their sins and those for their afflictions. This intimates that he observes them with compassion and tender concern; he is afflicted in their afflictions, and knows their souls in adversity . . . . Paul was mindful of Timothy's tears (2 Timothy 1:4), and God will not forget the sorrows of his people . . . . God will comfort his people according to the time wherein he has afflicted them, and give to those to reap in joy who sowed in tears. What was sown as a tear will come up a pearl.

But the glorious prospect is that God is to break His tear bottle, and wipe away all the tears of His sorrowing children. No eyes will ever be stained with tears in heaven, simply because there are no trials and losses there to weep over. As E. Stanley Jones expresses it:

> Sin, suffering, and death are negatives; goodness, joy, and life are positives. The first three are a trinity of denials, the last three are a trinity of affirmations. The future, then, lies with these affirmations, no matter what the present word spoken may say. We believe that sin, suffering, and death will be banished from the universe with the ultimate triumph of the kingdom of God.

An old proverb has it, "As soon as I was born, I wept, and every day shows why." Another has it, "We are born crying, live complaining, and die disappointed." Saints, however, although born crying, do not live complaining and die disappointed. They live and die in the assurance that their eternity will be one without crying. It is here that we can understand the way aged John described the Glory Land, the vision of which was given him by the Spirit on that unforgettable Lord's Day.

First of all, we have the glorious repeated positive: ". . . God will wipe away every tear from their eyes" (Revelation 7:17; 21:4 RSV). Why are these words, unequaled in their combined depth and tenderness, repeated? Usually in Scripture, repetition means emphasis. In the first reference, the millennial condition is in question when, for a thousand years, tears will be shed, and so the promise is future. In the latter reference, the heavenly land is portrayed by John. But the happy and assured portion of all God's people, heavenly and earthly, is that of "everlasting consolation." In both verses it will be noted that it is *God*, not the Lamb, who wipes away every tear. As He was the first sinned against, and, as a result, suffering entered the world, He it is who removes all causes and occasions of sorrow.

There are no wet eyes in heaven, but in hell, tears forever fall. Lazarus, the poor, suffering pauper, reclines peacefully in Abraham's bosom, but the rich man lifts up his tear-filled eyes in torment in hell.

But John goes on to give us an array of assuring negatives of what will be missing from "the land of pure delight, where saints immortal reign."

No death. John affirms that death shall not exist any more (21:4). Only in the eternal state are the effects of sin, physical and moral, radically removed. God removes every cause and occasion of sorrow. Death that came through sin, has been responsible for more tears than any other cause. But God will wipe every eye dry, and we will never again weep over the death of those we love, for there are no funerals or graves in heaven. Physical death exists no more.

> Death, like a narrow sea, divides
> This heavenly land from ours.
>
> ISAAC WATTS

Now, death divides us, breaks up our homes, and causes our hearts and eyes to become fountains of sorrow; but "death's cold flood" does not "freight us from the shore," for in heaven we shall be like Him who, by dying, slew death—*alive for evermore!*

No grief. John uses this same word in Revelation 18:15, as "wailing," or mourning, the outward expression of the heart's deep anguish. We read of the grief of God, of Christ, and of the Spirit because of our sins, and it pleased the Father to put His Son to grief that salvation from sin might be ours. Although saved by His matchless grace, there is much in the world responsible for our personal grief. But how wonderful it will be never to know heart grief again, never to cause or receive anguish of mind again.

No crying. The word Isaiah uses for *crying* implies the voice of hopeless misery. But in the creation of the new heavens and the new earth, all former crying will be forgotten. A child enters the world crying, cries its way through life, and has many loved ones crying when it comes to leave the world. In heaven, God has His "people a joy" and finds "joy in them." Thus "the voice of weeping" is heard no more in the land of pure delight (*see* Isaiah 65:17–19).

No distress. This further negative is associated
with pain within, or from without, caused by internal
trouble or external adverse circumstances. All that
goes to make up the volume of human misery no
longer exists, because the sin responsible for it cannot
pollute heaven, into which nothing that defiles can
enter.

"*. . . the former things are passed away*" (Revelation
21:4). These "things" cover, not only those just
mentioned, but all things alien to the will of God, and
responsible for man's anguish, sorrow, and sin here
below. Let us not be misunderstood when we mention
grief and glory together. In more than one Bible
verse the two appear in close company, having been
written probably with the same dipping of pen. "Ob-
servation bears it out that most of the things that have
come to have a glory about them also had, some-
where, suffering associated with them, with the glory,
however, eventually outweighing the suffering." Paul,
however, had more in mind than glorying in his infirmities, and of the spiritual gains from such when he
wrote to the Romans:

> I consider that the sufferings of *this present
> time* are not worth comparing with the glory
> that is to be revealed in us.
>
> 8:18 RSV, italics added

This, surely, is the glory yet to follow.

In his forceful contrast between this life and all

its enigmas, and the life to come with its perfect satisfaction, Paul uses two short, simple words—*now* and *then* (1 Corinthians 13:9–13).

> *Now* we see through a glass darkly.
> *Now* we know in part.
>
> *Then* face to face.
> *Then* shall I know.

As Paul, and other writers, found consolation in balancing the one with the other, so can we, if only we constantly remember the words of earth's most illustrious Sufferer. ". . . What I do thou knowest not now; but thou shalt know hereafter."

Doctor Stuart Holden used to tell of an experience he had when visiting a factory where cloth was woven. "I well remember a visit to a factory where fine linen damask was being woven. As I watched a weaver at his loom, I was perplexed as to how the pattern, which slowly grew before one's eyes as the shuttles went backward and forward, was formed and directed. In reply to my enquiry the weaver pointed overhead to where a seemingly complex arrangement of perforated cards was suspended. This kept moving upward and downward in evident unison with the lateral movements of the shuttles. Obviously, even to one so technically ignorant as myself, there was some connection between them. And, laconically, the weaver said, pointing as he spoke, 'Pattern's up *there!*' "

We must not forget that the pattern we fail to see of our perplexities is up there—a pattern fashioned by divine love and wrought out by divine wisdom. When the loom is silent and the shuttles cease to fly, then the Weaver will explain why the dark threads were as needful as the threads of gold and silver. As the skies continue dark and overcast, and shades of night obscure the light, may grace be ours ever to remember that the God who cannot err is able to make us perfect through suffering.

George Matheson reminds us there is a "joy that seeketh us through pain." With our finite minds we are not wise enough to understand all that is best for us; but our Lord does, seeing He is Alpha and Omega and all in between, and we are gathered up in His loving arms.

John Ruskin wrote a meaningful short essay he called *The Music of a Rest:*

> "There is no music in a rest" but there is the making of music in it. In our whole life-melody the music is broken off here and there by rests and we foolishly think we have come to the end of the theme. God sends a time of forced leisure, sickness, disappointed plans, frustrated efforts, and makes a sudden pause in the choral hymn of our loves;

and we lament that our voices must be silent, and our part missing in the music which ever goes up to the ear of the Creator. How does the musician read the rest? See him beat the time with unvarying count, and catch up the next note true and steady, as if no breaking place had come between.

Not without design does God write the music of our lives. Be it ours to learn the tune, and not to be dismayed at the rests. They are not to be slurred over, not to be omitted, not to destroy the melody, not to change the keynote. If we look up, God Himself will beat the time for us. With the eye on Him, we shall strike the next note full and clear. If we sadly say to ourselves, there is no music in a rest, let us not forget there is the making of music in it. The making of music is often a slow and painful process in this life. How patiently God works to teach. How long He waits for us to learn the lesson.

As we know, there are many who bear indelible tokens of physical, mental, or material sufferings. But, with death, all the scars disappear as the body returns to dust and ashes. In the new body awaiting the child of God, a body not made with hands, eternal in the heavens, such visible marks will not be possible, seeing it will be a body without sin, and therefore without all the ravages of suffering. Such a spiritual body will be perfect, and consequently painless and scarless.

The only One in heaven who carries in His glorified body the former earthly stigmata of suffering is our blessed Lord. When we see Him, we will not ask, "What are these wounds in Thine hands?" We will know that we are in heaven because of them, and that those visible nail prints abide as an eternal reminder of the price paid for our redemption, and for the privilege of sharing His Father's home with Him.

The wounds of His hands, feet, and side are forever a part of His glorified body. He rose from the grave with them, and with them He ascended into heaven. If we could see, they are visible today above, and will be throughout eternity. The third verse of Matthew Bridges's remarkable hymn *Crown Him With Many Crowns,* reads:

> Crown Him the Lord of love:
> Behold His hands, and side,
> Rich wounds, yet visible above,
> In beauty glorified:
> No angel in the sky
> Can fully bear that sight,
> But downward bends His burning eye
> At mysteries so bright.

When John came to describe Christ in His kingly character, he tells us that he saw Him standing as "a Lamb as it had been slain" (*see* Revelation 5:6). The thought conveyed is that of being freshly slain. Thus the wound prints the disciples beheld are seen again by John in his Master's glorified body in heaven, proving that the memories of Calvary are treasured in heaven. The center of heaven's glory is the Lamb that was slain, still bearing the scars of the cross.

We have had much to say about the ominous silence of God in our suffering. What we have to learn is how to be silent before Him in all that He, in His infinite wisdom, permits to overtake us. "In every thing give thanks . . ." (1 Thessalonians 5:18). It will be noted that Paul did not say *"For* everything give thanks" but *"in* everything." When pain, losses, reverses overtake us, it seems out of season to bless God for the experiences that hurt and bleed, yet *in* them we can bless God that all things are arranged for His redeemed children by His wisdom, are pendent on His will, sanctified by His blessing, according with His promises, and flowing from His love. We may not understand the meaning of our tears, but He who knows best, does, and for this we should give thanks. The end always justifies the means He employs to make us more like Himself.

A proverb reminds us that we "fear to suffer, as well as suffer from fear" and such fear destroys faith in God's beneficent purposes our sufferings seem to obscure. As Jesus entered the final phase of His extreme anguish at Calvary, deserted by men and seemingly by God, the heartless crowd cried, "He trusted in God; let him deliver him now, if he will have him . . ." (Matthew 27:43). Their implication was that if God did miraculously deliver His Son, it would be a public proof that He was holy, and pleasing to His Father; but if God permitted His beloved Son to die such an ignominious death, then it was sure proof that His Father did not desire Him.

We do not say that God can't intervene when His own suffer—He can and does according to His wisdom. What we should avoid is affirming that God should intervene in impending suffering and calamity whenever His children face such; and that if He does intervene, it is a special sign of His being pleased with them; and that if He does not step in at the crucial moment, something is wrong with God or with themselves. It is because that we, too, are perfected through our sufferings, that our loving heavenly Father permits and adjusts them accordingly. We are assured that the trial of our faith is much more precious than gold that perishes. We may shrink from the fiery trial but the promise is ours that the Lord is with us in the furnace—just as He was with the three Hebrew youths long ago—to preserve us, even as He protected them. Thus, in every hour of trial we must learn to sing with a peaceful heart, *He knows! He knows!* Some bright day when the canvas is unrolled and we see the perfect pattern the divine Weaver sketched for each of us, then "We'll bless the Hand that guided, And the Heart that planned."

As we continue living in a world with its problems of human suffering, may we be found sharing the confidence of Daniel who by divine inspiration looked down the vista of the ages and declared:

> . . . he [God] doeth according to his will in the army of heaven, and among the inhabitants of the earth: and none can stay his hand, or say unto him, What doest thou?
>
> Daniel 4:35